W9-AKB-724

VANDERBILT UNIVERSITY LIBRARY

The Iroquois

MICHELLE LOMBERG

PRINCIPAL PHOTOGRAPHY BY MARILYN "ANGEL" WYNN

CHELSEA CLUBHOUSE

An Imprint of Chelsea House Publishers

A Haights Cross Communications Company

Philadelphia

3 1489 00501 7783

#1695 B+T

FREEPORT MEMORIAL LIBRARY

This edition first published in 2004 in the United States of America by Chelsea Clubhouse, a division of Chelsea House Publishers and a subsidiary of Haights Cross Communications.

All rights reserved. No part of this publication may be reproduced or transmitted in any form or by any means without the written permission of the publisher.

Chelsea Clubhouse
1974 Sproul Road, Suite 400
Broomall, PA 19008-0914

The Chelsea House world wide web address is www.chelseahouse.com

Library of Congress Cataloging-in-Publication Data

Lomberg, Michelle.
  The Iroquois / Michelle Lomberg.
     v. cm. -- (American Indian art and culture)
Includes bibliographical references and index.
Contents: The people -- Iroquois homes -- Iroquois communities --
Iroquois clothing -- Iroquois food -- Tools and technology -- Iroquois
religion -- Ceremonies and celebrations -- Music and dance -- Language
and storytelling -- Iroquois art -- Special feature -- Studying the
Iroquois' past.
  ISBN 0-7910-7965-1 (Chelsea House) (lib. bdg. : alk. paper)
  1. Iroquois Indians--History--Juvenile literature. 2. Iroquois
Indians--Social life and customs--Juvenile literature. [1. Iroquois
Indians.] I. Title. II. Series.
  E99.I7L65 2004
  974.7004'9755--dc22

                          2003017522
                Printed in the United States of America
                1 2 3 4 5 6 7 8 9 0   07 06 05 04 03

©2004 WEIGL EDUCATIONAL PUBLISHERS LIMITED

Project Coordinator Heather C. Hudak **Copy Editor** Donald Wells **Design** Janine Vangool
Layout Terry Paulhus **Photo Researcher** Wendy Cosh **Chelsea Clubhouse Editors** Sally Cheney
and Margaret Brierton **Validator** Mike "Wahrare" Tarbell

Cover: Iroquois Village (Marilyn "Angel" Wynn), Iroquois Woman (Marilyn "Angel" Wynn), Iroquois Tribal Flag (Marilyn "Angel" Wynn), Iroquois Tododaho (Marilyn "Angel" Wynn); Kit Breen: pages 5, 18, 22; Courtesy of Melanie Printup Hope: page 27; Jan Lucie: page 20; Marilyn "Angel" Wynn: pages 1, 3, 6, 7, 8, 9, 10L, 10R, 11T, 11B, 12/13, 13T, 14T, 14B, 15, 16, 17, 19, 21T, 21B, 23, 24T, 24B, 25, 26T, 26B, 28T, 28B, 29, 30, 31.

Please note
At the time of printing, the Internet addresses appearing in this book were correct. Owing to the dynamic nature of the Internet, however, we cannot guarantee that all these addresses will remain correct.

CONTENTS

The People

The Iroquois call themselves *Haudenosaunee*, which means "people who live in the extended **longhouse**." Their **Algonquin** enemies gave them the name Iroquois. In Algonquin, the word *Iroquois* means "rattlesnakes." European settlers also used the word Iroquois to refer to this American Indian group.

Hundreds of years ago, five American Indian nations came together to create one of the world's first **democracies**. This was known as the Iroquois **Confederacy**. This confederacy was formed by the Mohawk, Oneida, Onondaga, Cayuga, and Seneca nations around 1570. The Tuscarora joined the confederacy in 1722.

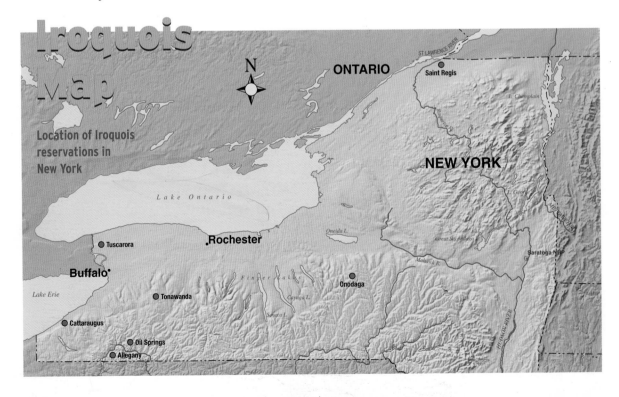

Iroquois Map

Location of Iroquois reservations in New York

Each nation in the Iroquois Confederacy had its own culture, land, and traditions. These different elements of each group's history were combined to create the Iroquois culture.

The confederacy maintained peace among its members. It also offered each nation help and protection from both warring European settlers and attacks from other American Indian groups who might attack. The Iroquois thought of the confederacy as an imaginary longhouse that reached from the Mohawk lands in the east to the Seneca lands in the west.

Songs and dances are used to explain the history and culture of the Iroquois people.

The Mohawk lived in New York. They were the first nation of the Iroquois Confederacy. They were called the Eastern Door Keepers because they protected the confederacy from any dangers that might approach along the eastern border of Iroquois lands.

The Oneida lived in central New York and Canada. The Oneida Nation was the smallest group in the Iroquois Confederacy.

The Onondaga lived near Syracuse, New York–the center of the Iroquois Confederacy. They hosted the annual meeting of the confederacy.

The Cayuga lived along Cayuga Lake in New York. Chief Big Pipe was the leader of the Cayuga when they joined the confederacy, so they are also known as the People of the Pipe.

The Seneca lived south of Lake Ontario, between Lake Erie and Seneca Lake. The Seneca Nation was the largest group in the Iroquois Confederacy.

In the early 1700s, the Tuscarora migrated from North Carolina to New York. The Tuscarora joined the confederacy in 1722.

Iroquois Homes

The longhouse was the center of Iroquois life. Longhouses were long, narrow buildings with arched roofs. Low porches covered the doorways, which were located at both ends of the longhouse.

To build a longhouse, men tied long wooden poles together to form arches. Then they placed the poles lengthwise to connect and support the arches. Large shingles made of elm bark covered the whole structure. Longhouses lasted about 20 years before they began to rot.

By the 1740s, many of the Iroquois lived in longhouses made from logs rather than bark.

DWELLING AND DECORATION

A long aisle, about 10 feet (3 meters) wide, ran through the center of the longhouse. Inside, the longhouse was divided into apartments. Each apartment was 20 feet (6.1 meters) long and housed two families. About 20 families lived in one longhouse. These families shared the fires that were built in the center of the aisle.

Longhouse dwellers used their space well. For example, families kept their belongings in storage closets. They neatly hung items, such as snowshoes, on walls. They hung corn and other foods from the ceiling to dry. The Iroquois built platforms along the interior walls of the longhouse. They used these platforms for sitting and sleeping. The Iroquois covered themselves with mats and furs to keep warm. Mats and furs also lined the longhouse walls, providing insulation from the cold.

Longhouses were usually between 60 and 220 feet (18 and 67 meters) long. Some were as long as 400 feet (122 meters). Most longhouses were 20 feet (6.1 meters) wide and 20 feet (6.1 meters) high.

Today, many Iroquois live in framed houses or trailers on reservation land. Some Iroquois farm the land, but most land remains in its natural state. Some Iroquois communities have built stores, schools, and banks to house some of the modern services that their residents require.

Iroquois Communities

Iroquois villages were organized under a **clan** system. In Iroquois culture, clans were **matrilineal**. Each Iroquois village had a minimum of three clans, which were named after an animal or a bird. Each Iroquois nation had a Turtle, Wolf, and Bear clan.

Each clan had its own longhouse. Families of the same clan lived together in these longhouses. Clan members worked together and shared resources. The oldest woman in a clan was the clan mother. She selected the chief of the clan. The chief represented the clan at village and tribal **councils**.

Each longhouse lasted about 10 to 20 years before a shortage of soil and firewood and a buildup of pests caused the Iroquois to build a new longhouse.

Chiefs were always men. The clan mother also named the children of the clan. This practice continues among many Iroquois families today.

Men and women had important jobs in the community. Men built longhouses. They made tools from stone, bone, and wood. They hunted animals, such as bear and deer. They fought wars and defended their villages from attackers. Women grew and preserved food. They cooked meals and made clothes. They also cared for young children. Both men and women helped make decisions that affected their community.

Children were an important part of Iroquois culture. Mothers and uncles taught children the skills they needed to survive as adults. Grandmothers and grandfathers told stories that taught the Iroquois children values and history. Today, most Iroquois communities have two types of government—elected and traditional.

People remained members of their clans for their entire lives. Clan members could not marry each other. When a couple married, the husband moved into his wife's longhouse, but he did not become a member of her clan. He remained a member of his mother's clan. Children born to the couple belonged to the mother's clan.

Senior members of the community teach Iroquois children to respect the land. Children learn how their actions will affect future generations.

Iroquois Clothing

Traditional Iroquois clothing was both useful and beautiful. Iroquois women made clothes from deerskin. They sewed the clothes with bone needles, using **sinew** as thread. They decorated the clothes with porcupine quills and shell beads. Popular beadwork designs included flowers, leaves, and clan symbols. Strawberries were a popular symbol because they were the first fruit to bloom in the new year and they represented a new beginning.

Today, Iroquois women wear cloth dresses, which are decorated with porcupine quills or beadwork. Women always wear leggings underneath a dress or skirt.

Iroquois men usually wore fringed deerskin shirts, but in hot weather, Iroquois men wore deerskin **sashes** instead of shirts. They also made sashes from plant fibers by weaving the fibers together.

Iroquois men wore feathered hats, which were decorated with porcupine quills or wampum beads.

Men wore leggings and breechcloths to cover their lower bodies. These items were made of deerskin with fringed edges. Men often wore hats that were decorated with feathers, beads, and porcupine quills.

Women wore deerskin dresses, skirts, and leggings. Sometimes, they wore belts or sashes around their waists. Women also wore beautiful beaded headbands.

Both men and women wore deerskin **moccasins**. Iroquois moccasins were cuffed at the ankle. They decorated the cuff and the top of the moccasin with porcupine quills or shell beads. The Iroquois were also known to make shoes from braided cornhusks.

As the Iroquois began to trade with Europeans, they acquired materials such as cloth, glass beads, and ribbon. They incorporated these items into traditional clothing. Today, Iroquois people wear store-bought clothes. However, they still use **calico** to make traditional clothing, such as shirts, dresses, skirts, and sashes. They decorate these items with beads and silver **broaches**.

The Iroquois often attached beaded fabric to their moccasins. When the moccasins wore out, the fabric was removed and attached to a new pair.

Iroquois Food

The Iroquois diet consisted mainly of corn, beans, and squash. These foods were known as the Three Sisters. They were planted, eaten, and celebrated together. The women grew all of their crops in one field to promote plant growth. For example, tall cornstalks acted as poles to support bean vines. The bean plants nourished the soil. Low-lying squash plants kept the ground moist and prevented weeds from growing.

Women and girls preserved food for winter. They roasted and dried ears of corn. They ground some of this corn into cornmeal. They also smoked and dried meat and fish. In summer, they stored fresh food in underground pits. The cool temperature in these pits kept food from rotting.

The Iroquois usually ate one meal a day. That meal was often soup made from meat and vegetables. **Venison** was one of the main meats the Iroquois ate. Iroquois men hunted bear, beaver, and moose, too. Men also caught fish using spears, hooks, and traps. Boys hunted small game, such as rabbits and birds.

With an adult, try making this Mohawk recipe.

Iroquois women gathered berries, nuts, mushrooms, greens, and other foods that grew in the woods.

Mohawk Corn Bread

Ingredients:

1 pound corn flour

2 cups (473.2 ml) canned kidney beans

salt to taste

water

Equipment:

large bowl

wooden spoon

large pot

slotted spoon

butter knife

1. Mix the flour, beans, and salt with some water. Add enough water to create a stiff dough.

2. Mold the dough into round patties. Each patty should be about 6 inches (15.2 centimeters) wide and 2 inches (5 centimeters) thick.

3. With an adult's help, carefully place the patties in boiling water. After about 1 hour, the patties will rise to the top of the water.

4. Ask an adult to help you remove the patties from the water using a slotted spoon. Let the patties cool.

5. Use a butter knife to butter a patty. For a traditional meal, serve the corn bread patties with squash. Corn bread patties can also be served with maple syrup.

Tools, Weapons, and Defense

The Iroquois used tools to hunt and fish. They also used tools to build longhouses and canoes, prepare food, and make clothing.

Iroquois building tools included axes, adzes, and chisels. Axe heads were made of stone, which was ground and polished against other stones to make it sharp. The axe head fit inside a wooden handle. An adze was a tool they used to chop down trees and shape wood. Adzes also had stone heads and wooden handles. The Iroquois used stone or antler chisels to peel bark from logs, too.

Iroquois women used tools to grow and prepare food. They used pointed digging sticks to plant crops. They ground corn using a mortar and pestle. The mortar was made from a length of tree trunk that had a shallow dish carved in the top. The pestle was a heavy, blunt piece of wood.

Iroquois women needed many tools to make clothing. Women used stone and bone scrapers to remove flesh from animal hides. Bone tools called awls were used to punch holes for sewing. Bone needles drew sinew through the holes.

The Iroquois made farming tools, such as rakes, from deer antlers.

The Iroquois attached arrow points to straight sticks to make a sharp arrow.

HUNTING TOOLS AND WAR WEAPONS

Iroquois men hunted large and small game with bows and arrows. Arrowheads were made of **flint**. Flint is a stone that can be chipped to form a sharp point. The Iroquois also used a variety of traps made of wood, rawhide, and sinew to catch animals, birds, and fish.

The Iroquois also used bows and arrows to fight wars. They also used war clubs, which were heavy wooden sticks with a round, knobby ball at one end. High fences made of pointed poles were another wartime tool that prevented attackers from reaching Iroquois villages. They called these fences palisades.

In the 1600s, the Iroquois began using guns for hunting and fighting. They acquired guns from European traders. The Europeans introduced other metal goods, such as knives and kettles, to the Iroquois, too.

Women put dry corn kernels inside the dish of the mortar and pounded the kernels with the pestle.

Iroquois Religion

Religion was an important part of traditional Iroquois life. Religious beliefs varied from nation to nation. The Iroquois believed that everything around them had a spirit. These spirits controlled the weather, crops, and animals. Most Iroquois believed in a powerful creator named the Great Spirit. The Iroquois performed several rituals and ceremonies to give thanks to the Great Spirit. The Iroquois believed the Great Spirit had an evil twin brother who caused mischief and suffering.

The medicine wheel is often used during celebrations. Each stone of the medicine wheel represents part of the story of creation. The circle represents the life cycle.

Medicine and religion were closely tied in Iroquois culture. Medicine societies were groups of people who performed special rituals to heal the sick and bring well-being to the nation. Medicine rituals often involved singing and dancing. During some rituals, the participants wore masks made of wood or cornhusks. The Iroquois believed these masks had great spiritual power.

During the harvest season, the Iroquois used cornhusk masks to give thanks for plentiful crops.

CREATION

Before the world was created, Sky Woman and Sky Man lived on an island in the sky. One day, Sky Man uprooted a tree, leaving a hole in the island. Sky Woman fell through the hole. She fell toward Earth, which was covered with water. As she fell, the animals on Earth tried to save her. To ease her fall, two birds caught Sky Woman on their backs. A frog dove to the bottom of the water to get mud to soften her landing. He placed the mud on a turtle's back. The frog continued to place mud on the turtle's back. Soon, there was so much mud on the turtle's back that the continent of North America formed. The Iroquois call North America Turtle Island.

One day, Sky Woman gave birth to twin boys. One twin was good, and the other was evil. The good twin was worshiped as the Great Spirit. He created all that is good on Earth. The evil twin created all that is bad.

Ceremonies and Celebrations

The Iroquois often gathered to celebrate and give thanks for the gifts of the Great Spirit. Ceremonies honored different harvests and events throughout the year.

One of the many Iroquois celebrations was the Green Corn Festival, which is the oldest Iroquois ceremony. This festival was celebrated every year at the beginning of the corn harvest in August. The Green Corn Festival lasted several days. There were speeches of thanks and offerings of tobacco to the Great Spirit. There were also dances, feasts, and games. The Iroquois celebrated the end of the corn harvest with the Harvest Festival.

The Iroquois perform traditional dances during ceremonies and celebrations.

The largest Iroquois celebration was the Midwinter Festival. The 6-day festival was celebrated at the beginning of the new year to give thanks to the Creator. People prepared for the festival by cleaning their longhouses. They also talked about their dreams and how those dreams had guided them through the past year. When the festival began, people visited each other's longhouses to stir the fire ashes inside. Stirring the ashes was symbolic of renewal. They scattered the fire of the old year before the new fires were lit. This festival featured feasts, dances, and games.

Other celebrations included the Maple Festival, the Planting Ceremony, the Thunder Ceremony, and the Strawberry Festival.

When they were not working or celebrating, the Iroquois enjoyed playing games. They played the Bowl Game using a bowl filled with six plum or peach stones. The stones were painted black on one side. Players bet whether the dark or light sides of the stones would face upward when the bowl was banged on the ground. The Iroquois also enjoyed sports like **lacrosse** and stickball, which were similar to what is now known as field hockey. Another popular sport was Snow Snake. In this game, players competed to see who could slide a long stick farthest across the snow.

Lacrosse is one of the fastest growing team sports in the United States and Europe.

Music and Dance

Iroquois of all ages enjoyed social dances. Both men and women danced. Some dances were performed by men. Other dances were performed by women. Dancers kept time to a beat played on drums and rattles. The Iroquois made water drums from clay pots that were covered with hide. The drums were filled with water to improve their sound. Rattles were made from horns, deer hoofs, or turtle shells.

Dancers moved in a counter-clockwise circle, stomping or shuffling their feet. During some dances, dancers challenged each other to dance more quickly as the drumbeat became faster.

Singing, dancing, and playing musical instruments has always been an important part of Iroquois celebrations and religious ceremonies.

CEREMONIAL DANCING

Both men and women performed the Round Dance. As many as ten singers sat in the center of a circle. Water drums and rattles accompanied their singing. Women led the dance, and men joined in later. Dancers stepped sideways, one foot at a time. When the rhythm changed, the dancers changed direction.

The Iroquois still enjoy traditional dances. Iroquois and other American Indians host powwows throughout the year. A powwow is a gathering that includes music, dance, food, gifts, and souvenirs. People compete in singing, drumming, and dancing contests.

The water drum was made from a hollowed log. Water was placed in the bottom of the log before rawhide was stretched over the top.

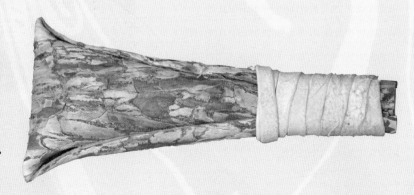

The Iroquois made elm bark rattles. They placed small stones and pebbles inside the bark so the rattle would make a noise.

Language and Storytelling

The languages of all six Iroquois nations belong to the Iroquoian language family. These languages are similar, but they are not the same. The Iroquois had no written language. They used images to record history. They wove these images onto beaded wampum belts.

Iroquoian languages were very expressive. Gifted speakers gained respect for their **wit** and **persuasive** power. Clan mothers selected chiefs based on their **oratory** skill. In the Iroquois Confederacy, chiefs of the six nations had to agree **unanimously** on all decisions. Chiefs would make speeches to convince other chiefs to support their decisions.

Storytelling was an important activity in Iroquois culture. When families gathered around longhouse fires, elders told stories. Some stories explained the history of the Iroquois Confederacy. Other stories were about the creation of the natural

Iroquois storytellers pass on cultural traditions through oral histories.

world. Some stories demonstrated the difference between good and bad behavior.

Today, many Iroquois are trying to preserve their languages. Beginning in the 1800s, the U.S. government sent American Indian children to **boarding schools**. Students learned to speak English at these schools. They were not allowed to speak their own languages. As a result, several generations of Iroquois children did not learn to speak their own language. Today, Iroquois children are no longer sent to boarding schools to learn English. Many Iroquois are learning the Iroquoian languages to preserve this part of their culture.

Hiawatha was an Onondaga chief who convinced the other nations of the Iroquois Confederacy to make peace. The tale of Hiawatha is often told by Iroquois storytellers.

MONTHS

In the Mohawk language, the names of months are descriptive. They reflect the weather and the agricultural cycle.

January Tsiothohrko:wa
Very Cold Moon

February Enniska
Mid-winter Moon

March Ennisko:wa
Sugar Moon

April Onearahtokha
Fishing Moon

May Onerahtohko:wa
Planting Moon

June Ohiariha
Strawberry Moon

July Onhiarihko:wa
Blueberry (Green Bean) Moon

August Seskeha
Green Corn Moon

September Seskehko:wa
Freshness Moon

October Kentenha
Harvest Moon

November Kentenko:wa
Hunting Moon

December Tsiothohrha
Cold Moon

Iroquois Art

Traditional Iroquois culture was filled with art. The Iroquois decorated clothing with porcupine quills or shell beads that were beautifully arranged. Striking geometric patterns were woven into baskets. They used fine clay pots for storing, cooking, and serving food.

Iroquois women used special techniques to make pots. First, the potter ensured the clay was clean. Then she added crushed rocks to harden the clay. Iroquois women used their hands and simple tools to shape pots.

While the clay was still damp, the potter pressed or scratched designs onto the surface of the clay. The pots were dried in the Sun. Then the pots were baked in a fire.

Basketmaker Mary Kawennatakie Adams designed the Pope Basket as a gift for the Pope.

Iroquois mothers give the faceless corn husk doll to their children to teach them that the way they look is not as important as who they are.

Art also had a spiritual role in Iroquois culture. Men carved elaborate masks for the False Face Society. The False Face Society used masks as part of a ritual to cure illnesses. The masks were carved on living trees. Once complete, the masks were cut from the tree. These masks were sacred objects. Many Iroquois people considered it disrespectful to show photos of the masks or to display them in public.

Today, some Iroquois create art to preserve their culture. They also earn their income by selling their art. Iroquois beadwork has always been admired. Beadworkers have adapted their work over time. Since the 1800s, Iroquois women have beaded souvenir items to sell to tourists. Today, Iroquois beadwork is displayed in galleries and private collections. Iroquois women sell their art at powwows, souvenir shops, and on the Internet.

The Iroquois peeled bark from elm trees in the spring and early summer. They bent the bark to make trays and bowls.

Wampum

Wampum has a spiritual meaning in the Iroquois culture. Wampum belts are made by weaving strings of white and purple shell beads into a long strip. The white beads represent peace and harmony. The purple beads symbolize hostility and destruction. The Iroquois used shell beads to create simple shapes. These shapes told stories. Long ago, the Iroquois used wampum belts to record important events or send messages.

Women wove wampum belts by hand and on small **looms**. They strung the beads onto thread made from plant fiber. They wove the threaded beads into long strips of leather or sinew.

Wampum belts had many uses. They were used to invite chiefs to councils. Wampum belts were also traded and given as gifts. A man's family would give a wampum belt to the family of the woman he wanted to marry. If the woman's family accepted the belt, the couple was engaged. The founding of the Iroquois Confederacy is recorded on a wampum belt, too.

Europeans thought wampum belts were money. They used wampum as a form of currency when trading with American Indians.

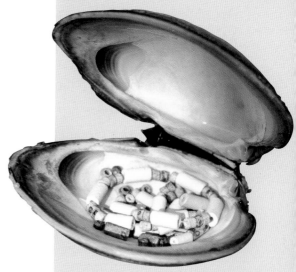

The Iroquois made wampum beads by cutting and grinding shells into bead shapes. Sharp stones were used to drill through the beads.

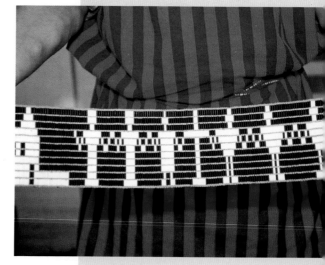

MODERN ARTIST

Melanie Printup Hope

Melanie Printup Hope is an Iroquois digital and installation artist. She was raised on the Tuscarora Indian Reservation in western New York. Hope studied graphic design at the Rochester Institute of Technology in New York. Later, she earned a Master of Fine Arts degree from Rensselaer Polytechnic Institute, where she studied electronic arts.

Hope uses her art to explore her American Indian identity. Some of her art deals with political issues affecting Native peoples. Hope's art combines the traditions of the longhouse with the most modern artistic forms. She uses many different methods in her art. These include traditional beadwork, drawing, computer animation, digitized sound, and video. Some of Hope's work is in video format. Other works are installations. Installations are complete settings that the viewer can see, hear, touch, and walk around.

Hope's work has been shown across North America and as far away as Belgium. She has received several awards, including fellowships from the Rockefeller Foundation and the National Endowment for the Arts.

Hope is a graphic designer as well as a fine artist. She teaches design at Sage College in Albany, New York, where she is an assistant professor. Hope has also taught at the Rensselaer Polytechnic Institute, Skidmore College in New York State, and the Banff Center for the Arts in Canada.

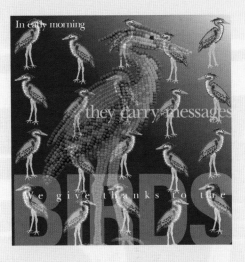

Some of Hope's work can be seen on the Internet.

Studying the Iroquois' Past

Archaeologists must search carefully to find traces of Iroquois villages. By carefully searching, archaeologists have found remains of 600-year-old Iroquois villages. Iroquois artifacts are some of the hardest to find. Unlike other American Indians, the Iroquois often use materials from plants and animals, which decay over time.

Since Iroquois longhouses were made of wood, over time, they would rot away. By looking carefully beneath the surface of the soil, archaeologists can see where a longhouse once stood. The wooden posts that once supported the longhouse leave round stains in the dirt. These stains are called post molds. By examining post molds, archaeologists can tell the size of the longhouse. They can also see where apartments and storage areas were located. Archaeologists can see where fires were built inside the longhouse. The soil where the hearth was located appears reddish in color. By counting the hearths, archaeologists can estimate how many people lived in the longhouse.

Archaeologists also read the writings of Europeans who visited longhouses. Some explorers kept detailed notes about Iroquois life.

Archaeologists use traditional Iroquois art and clothing, such as the glengarry cap, to determine how the culture lived hundreds of years ago.

TIME LINE

Late Woodland Period 1500 B.C. – A.D. 1300

American Indians in the Upper Great Lakes region begin making pottery. Iroquois culture in New York region begins to develop. Iroquois begin growing corn, beans, squash, pumpkins, and sunflowers.

Contact Period 1500 – 1600

Founding of the Iroquois Confederacy

Modern Period 1600 – present

There are ongoing wars against French and Huron. Traditional way of life declines. Many Iroquois settle in urban areas, such as Green Bay, Wisconsin. Men find jobs building bridges and skyscrapers.

Iroquois potters often used dark clay to make traditional shapes.

Make a Cornhusk Doll

Iroquois mothers made cornhusk dolls for their children. They dressed these dolls in traditional clothing. Corn silk was used to make soft hair for the dolls. When European settlers arrived in the United States, American Indians taught them how to make cornhusk dolls, too.

Materials

12 cornhusks	Scissors
Water	String

1. Soak the cornhusks in water until they are soft.

2. Arrange four cornhusks in layers. Place one cornhusk on the bottom. Place two cornhusks side-by-side in the center. Place one cornhusk on the top. The pointy end of the cornhusk should be facing down.

3. Tie the four cornhusks together about 2 inches (5 centimeters) from the top.

4. Use scissors to round the straight edges at the top of the cornhusks.

5. Turn the cornhusk bundle upside down. Pull the long husks over the trimmed edges.

6. Tie the end with string to form a ball. This is the doll's head.

7. Roll a cornhusk to form a narrow tube. This is the doll's arms. Tie the ends to form hands.

8. Place the arms between the cornhusks under the doll's head.

9. Tie the hanging cornhusks to make the doll's waist.

10. Make shoulders by draping a cornhusk behind the neck and crisscrossing the ends over the waist.

11. Arrange six cornhusks, flat side up, around the doll's waist to form a skirt. Tie the skirt and shoulders with string. You can also divide the skirt in two and tie string at the knees and ankles to make legs.

Further Reading

The Iroquois by Linda Bjornlund, Lucent Books, Inc., 2001, is part of the Indigenous Peoples of North America series. This book describes the traditional culture, religion, history, and modern life of the Iroquois.

People of the Dancing Sky: The Iroquois Way by Myron Zabol and Lorre Jensen (Stoddart, 2000) is a book of photographs. It shows modern Iroquois culture.

Web Sites

To learn more about the Iroquois way of life, navigate to "American Indians and the Natural World" by the Carnegie Museum of Natural History:
www.carnegiemuseums.org/cmnh/exhibits/north-south-east-west/iroquois/index.html

Listen to traditional Iroquois songs at:
www.ohwejagehka.com/songs.htm

Find out more about the six Iroquois nations at Peace 4 Turtle Island:
www.peace4turtleisland.org

To read the Constitution of the Iroquois Nations, visit:
www.constitution.org/cons/iroquois.htm

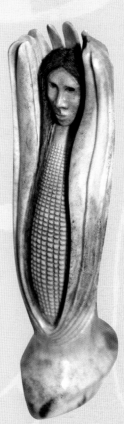

GLOSSARY

Algonquin: having to do with the Algonquin peoples, traditional enemies of the Iroquois

archaeologists: scientists who study objects from the past to learn about people who lived long ago

boarding schools: schools where children are sent to live and learn

broaches: large, decorative pins

calico: a heavy, brightly colored cloth

clan: a group of families related to each other

confederacy: a union or alliance of different groups

councils: meetings where people advise on, discuss, or organize something

democracies: governments in which decisions are made by the people or their chosen representatives

flint: a type of stone that can be shaped and sharpened

lacrosse: a sport played by throwing and catching a ball in a hand-held net

longhouse: a long, narrow house made of wood and bark

looms: tools used to make thread or yarn into cloth by weaving strands together

matrilineal: kinship that is traced through the mother's lines

moccasins: soft leather footwear that resembles slippers

oratory: the art of public speaking

persuasive: convincing someone to do something

sashes: strips of cloth or hide worn over one shoulder and fastened at the waist

sinew: tough fiber that joins muscle to bone

unanimously: with everyone agreeing

venison: deer meat

wit: keen

INDEX

DISCARDED BY
FREEPORT
MEMORIAL LIBRARY